Love of the Dark

Kira Carlin

BookLeaf Publishing

Presentation by *BookLeaf Publishing*

Web: www.bookleafpub.com

E-mail: info@bookleafpub.com

ISBN: 978-93-95755-25-2

First edition 2022

To Bubbus and Sarah, without whom I wouldn't write at all. You help me believe in the real kinds of love, and encourage me to be the most myself I can possibly be. You make me believe that I am, and always will be, enough.

Night Shift

She works the night shift too
I see her on the train
She always smiles at me
I try my best to smile back nicely
She makes me nervous
Like I could somehow screw up when I've
barely spoken a word
And still she smiles at me
She works close by
I try to practice my small talk
I love the way she laughs
Full-bodied with her head thrown back
We go on break at the same time
Find some creep to feed on
I crack open his skull
She smiles at me
"Thanks, sweetheart," she says before she drinks
his blood
I try not to freeze, try to look casual
I eat his brains
If my heart were beating, it would have skipped

Swim After Eating

I like to bring my kelpie things
Just some stuff I find around town
I like the way my kelpie sings
Even if the neighbours frown
My kelpie lives in the springs
And waters all around
They like what each evening brings
What new man that I have found
They could be paupers or kings
Of small or great renown
But I always find the ones with sins
Each of them a clown
When we get close to water, my kelpie grins
And pulls them all the way down
My kelpie wears many different skins
But always makes them drown

Maenad

I feel your love stir inside me
A passion that calls me to be
To be everything I am
Unapologetically
A love that leads me to feel
Truly feel
All of the bliss and despair
Allows me to scream and laugh
Makes space for my joy and rage
All in equal measure
Your worship is not of fear
Your altar is not hard stone
You demand sacrifice
Only by means of removing my shackles
Let my knife meet flesh
In devotion to you
And take revenge on those that keep us chained
And drink wine from their heads
We belong to no one
We are love
We are wrath
We are free

Puzzles Pieces

What a wonderful illusion it was
What perfect masks we wore
You were so desperate for love
But only if it looked the way it had been painted
in your head
Only if it moved in the way you had been told it
would
I was so desperate for a friend
That I would shove down all the unacceptable
parts of myself
Showing up for people in the hopes that they
would do the same for me
Save them from monsters in their heads
Hoping one day someone would help me with
mine
While still pretending mine didn't exist
But vampires wear charming smiles
Smiles that hide their sharp teeth
We sucked each other dry
The villain in each other's fairy tale
The dragon we have to slay
We both had puzzle pieces
Trying to make them fit
When we belong to different sets

Plane

I look up at the sky and think of him
The way he flew with silver wings
He is gone now, one year ago today
And I have nowhere to go
Nowhere to visit him
No grave for me to lay some flowers
Nowhere to stand to talk to him
All I have is my grief
And no one wants to talk about it
But I do
I want to talk about how he is gone
I want to grieve with someone
Someone who knew his quiet laugh
The cheeky gleam in his eye when he told a joke
I want to talk about how he loved to fly
When he took me up in a water plane on my
seventh birthday
How he changed
How I couldn't see him in those last few weeks
Because seeing the pain in his eyes
The way he didn't know who I was
Beyond knowing that he SHOULD know me
The way that gleam faded
I want to talk about how I can't see a plane
without thinking of him

How he would have told me the exact make
The type of engine
But no one wants to talk about it
As if silence will make it go away
But it never goes away
And I look at the sky and think of him

Friend

I feel so small beside you
Like a grain of dust
Who am I against centuries?
Against the rise and fall of empires?
Against all of history?
I pour out my heart in grief
Of lives not lived
Of people not dead
And I feel silly
Childish
But even after your ages of immortality
After everything seen and done
Your compassion burns bright
And your empathy has not worn down to apathy
You wipe the tears from my cheeks
Holding me tight
And I know what it means to have a true friend

Love Letter from a Sleep Paralysis Demon

Dark sheets covered the bed
Soft music plays on your phone
You toss and turn in your sleep
I wonder if you ever slept soundly
I know you're afraid
Afraid every moment
And even in sleep you don't find peace
You look tired every day
Through the false smiles and forced energy
I wish I could keep you here
And sometimes I try
I sit on your chest, weighing you down
I know you're afraid of me too
I see your eyes grow wide
They shine in the dark
You can't move
There's a lump in your throat as you hold your
breath
I'm holding you down
I just want you to sleep
When there is no one else here
When everyone is gone
Here I am
Waiting

Watching
It doesn't matter what you call me
I am always here
Even when you're scared to open your eyes
I am right there in front of you
I love you
Maybe not the way you want
But I know what you need
One day you will see
As I bind your arms and legs
And the paralysis takes you
It is my loving embrace
Urging you to rest
Rest now my darling
You need more sleep
Let me hold you down
And force your eyes shut
I hover above your face
Just inches away
I need to make sure
Are you sleeping soundly?
Or do you feel me there?
Even if you hate me
I will still be here
Loving you
Supporting you
Sleep
Don't open your eyes
Just sleep now
I will never leave you

Ariadne

I wasn't asleep
When I heard him creep away
Off to find something else
Or someone
To conquer
I felt it fully within me
The world of men
Hollowing me out
Until there was nothing left to take
Too tired to cry
I felt empty, numb
I begged for the island to take me
Let me sink into the ground
Sink into the ocean
Fall apart like sand
Washed away with the tide
I lay there for days
Just waiting for death
No home to return to
Ivy began to grow over me
I smiled, musing that the island really would
take me
I laughed
Softly at first
Then a chuckle

Then a cackle
It gave way to a sob
Which broke into a wail
I screamed
Roared with anger
Every emotion that I thought had left me
Burst through my chest with a force I had never
felt
I wanted to dance
I wanted to rend
A hand reached out to me
Behind it were soft eyes
Eyes that knew pain
Eyes that knew joy
Eyes so full of love and understanding
I felt tears sting my eyes
I squeezed that hand as tightly as I could
I had known monsters
So had they
And we knew all too well
The human faces monsters wore

The Little Things

Sometimes we sit inside all day
The sunlight filters in
I look over as you read in your chair
While I play games on the couch
You like to sit in the shade
You're always overheating
I sit in the sun because I'm always cold
It's perfect when we snuggle on the couch to
watch movies
Or in bed when I put my cold feet on your back
We shriek with laughter under bed sheets
You pull me closer and nibble on my ear
It tickles every time
You make me breakfast in bed
Brains have never tasted quite as good
As when you make them for me with scrambled
eggs

Back In Kind

A clear blue sky
So bright it burns
That clear blue sky
Holds forever
Just behind her eyes
She's a master thief
Pounding on my door
She walked right in
Asking what I could give
And without a second thought
I gave her everything
Eternity is a lonely sentence
And her company charmed me quickly
She saw beyond the shadows and fangs
She brought me sunlight
I gave her magic in return
The world belonged to her
My days and nights were warm
But the world was not worthy
The moment I turned my eyes away
The world pulled her to her knees
It tied her to a pyre
And spat on the gifts she offered
My ray of sunlight went up in smoke
And with it my compassion

If the world is to rob me of life
Then let me pay it back in kind
And yank every last drop of hope
And blood from every wretched leech
Until there is nothing left
As there is nothing left for me

Isolate at Home

My boyfriend brings the world to me
When I can't go outside
And even though I am trapped inside this house
The prison bars are harder to see when we're
cuddled on the bed
Even if I stay the same
There's no one I would rather watch grow old
I learn to love the prison cell
We make it a real home
Our friends call me old-fashioned when they
come to stay
They see me as a young man with vintage taste
They know I can never leave
So they take me on virtual tours
My boyfriend and I go on adventures with them
Every weekend over a video call
I died a long time ago
I'm trapped inside our home
I can't go out and see the world
But my boyfriend brings the world to me
And I don't feel alone

Death's Touch

I cannot touch you
I wish it were more simple
That neither of us would wither
But if I reached out my hand
You would be gone
And I would be alone again
But you say you need touch
Even when it is not something I can give
If I could just sit near you
If we could exist side by side
Couldn't that be enough?
But you demand my touch
Mortal life is so delicate
As I am, am I not enough?
If I touch you
That will be the end
I wish I could touch you
If only to put you at ease
But I can only touch you once
Just once as you go
And our incompatible love will end
I want my kind of love to be enough
To make you happy
Without asking me to be something I am not
I will never know your ache

And you will never know mine
And just before I hold you close
I will say goodbye

Bedtime

I smell the pine
Mixed in with the rain
I kept your clothes in the dryer
Along with a towel
You've been howling all night
Letting me know you're safe
Knowing I won't be able to sleep anyway
Not without you here
I'm a simple man
And I need to hold you close before I can rest
easy
I see your eyes
Glowing in the dark
I'm sure the full moon is up there somewhere
Hidden behind those dark rain clouds
You paw at the back door
Whining a little
With a fond smile I grab your towel from the
dryer
I call your name when I meet you at the door
And you stagger into my arms
You're dripping wet
I pull the warm towel around your shivering
frame
You may have less fur now

But I still feel the scruff on your face bristling
against my neck
I ruffle your hair with the towel
Feeling the soft chuckle in your chest
I help you into your warm clothes
Then into bed
You are tired, dear
Let's go to sleep
I kiss your brow
And hold you to my chest
My heart feels full too

Equivalent Exchange

They always ask me why
Why am I doing this
With all the things I could do
Why loose my wrath?
Why spit in the face of God?
I spent my life in service of Him
Why turn away now?
But I haven't turned away
My eyes are ever fixed
I face my target front on
And if I cannot go up to God
Then I will coax Him to me
I will destroy everything He loves
The world He supposedly holds dear
I will run rampant around the globe
Until there is not a single devoted worshipper
I will rend His churches asunder
I will crush His symbols
I will devour every warrior
And when there is no one left to love Him
Then He will know
He will know what He took
And the price that came with it

Cloudy Mornings

I love these cloudy mornings
Waking up tangled in your arms
When I can pull you close
And the covers stay warm
I can kiss your neck
Like a fresh cup of coffee
And you let me sink into you
Stormy weekend mornings
When you have nowhere to be
And I don't have to hide from the day
Eternity would blink by in seconds
If I could live like this with you forever

Cannibal Spirit

I feel your rage through the trees
Those burning eyes of coal
It was not your fault, my love
But I fear you've lost your soul

I wish that I could hold you close
Even as you eat their flesh
But your face has given way to bone
You like your victims fresh

I know you're in there somewhere
But I don't know where to start
If only I could heal you
And mend our broken hearts

I know those spirits took advantage
A second is all they seek
So that they could change you
They want you to be weak

But you were never weak to me
And I will always try
To bring you back home, darling
Even as I hear them cry
I wander out into those woods

I have to try and find you
I dare to speak your name
I know now what I have to do

Your anger causes you so much pain
It's lasted long enough
And as I walk towards you now
I know I must be tough

I do not fear you'll eat me now
You would have done so before
And I feel the bones upon the ground
The fresh and bloody gore

Give your heart again to me
My hand trembles against your chest
I'll cut that precious heart from you
And at last put you to rest

My tears are silent by the fire
Watching your heart burn
And this deep ache is rooted in my chest
For you, I still yearn

It was not your fault, my dear
I know this, lying in my grief
For the ache rattles in my bones
And I welcome the spirits with relief

Witch Love

They are the breath when the world feels too
much
The cool breeze that cuts through the heat
The wall I lean on
When I am unsure of what kind of man I am
They remind me
And when everything else is obscured
They alone are crystal clear
The fog clearing
The relief at the end of the day
My own witch
Bewitching me to forget my worries
To be under their spell is a welcome reprieve
Seducing me with their remedies
Their warm tea by the fireside
My magical love can cure all
And if I could create the same wonders with my
own voice
I would show them how they make the sun
brighter
How they make me feel strong enough to carry
the weight of life
But my voice is only a simple man's voice
And all it can do is whisper reverent prayers
To my witch

My love
And perhaps
Perhaps
Those prayers are enough

Banshee

I wanted to scream
Those brown eyes
So warm and eager
Those black lips smiling so softly
I felt my heart swell and break all at once
That warm touch that made my skin shiver
Excited and despairing
Her black sundress swayed
Above those chunky black boots
She walked like a celebration of death
Embracing the decay that gave the world life
She kissed like the world could end in the next
moment
And I wanted to scream
She was heaven
And I was haunted
Her brown skin felt better than silk
And I craved her touch like I was starving
Desperate to feel the life flowing through her
I should have screamed
Warned her that it was ending
That her life was about to be cut short
But I was as powerless against death as she was
And I wanted those moments to be real
To last without her impending doom

Persephone

I found love in the dark
In a world away from the one I was shackled to
It wasn't at all the way they tell you it is
Scary, painful, forced
No, love isn't like that at all
Not the kind of love you find when you are allowed
to just... Be
The love that demands nothing from you except
yourself
Your true, uncovered, unmasked, unmodified self
I found love in the dark and I ate it up
So hungry for the freedom to exist and explore
Without captivity or sheltering
I would have spent forever in the dark
Content in bliss I hadn't known in the light
Perpetually overfull after eating too much of a
favourite meal
After years of bland food without substance
But now that I know what love is in the dark
I need to find truth in the light
To let myself exist in both without the chains
To burst fully to life in all I can be
No matter where I go
Now I know my strength
Now I know love
Now I can be me

I'm The Ace You Throw Away

What kind of monster am I?
Barely able to talk, let alone love
But I do feel love
Just not the desired kind
Not the kind people want
Not the kind they demand
It is always too much and never enough
I am a zombie
Hungry, but never the right way
I am a vampire
No longer welcome over the thresholds of
homes I once knew
Because my love is never right
My body is decaying
The remains of my heart are partially eaten
Could you love a corpse?
Without needing things I can't give?
I have yearned for things for centuries
My love is fierce and bright
But is it good enough for you?
Can it be enough?
My love could turn me to ashes
Burning down like the sun
Could you allow a monster to love you?

Strike a bargain with a devil?
I am the monster people lie to
I am the monster people take from
Shuffling around aimlessly
I could be your best friend
A love more true than family
A love more true than sex
Could you love the kind of monster I am?
But these kinds of questions demand too much
And what kind of monster am I?

Midnight Picnics

They like to wonder what we do at night
What poor innocent victim we must be stalking
Or where we've hidden in the woods
Dancing and chanting, cursing some poor soul
I'm glad we're not that exciting
I much prefer our quiet nights
Sitting in the dark on the swing set
Smoking between coughs of laughter
Skinny dipping in the creek
Midnight picnics watching the planes fly
overhead
We have eternity to live our lives
And we make them well spent